The Dead Sea Poems

SIMON ARMITAGE

The Dead Sea Poems

faber and faber
LONDON · BOSTON

First published in Great Britain in 1995
by Faber and Faber Limited
3 Queen Square London WC1N 3AU

Phototypeset by Wilmaset Ltd, Wirral.
Printed in England by Clays Ltd, St Ives plc.

© Simon Armitage, 1995

Simon Armitage is hereby identified as author of this
work in accordance with Section 77 of the Copyright,
Designs and Patents Act 1988

A CIP record for this book
is available from the British Library

ISBN 0–571–17600–3

2 4 6 8 10 9 7 5 3

Contents

Acknowledgements

Acknowledgements and thanks are due to the editors of the following magazines in which many of these poems first appeared: *The Echo Room, Grand Street* (US), *The Guardian, The North, Poetry Review, Poetry Wales, The Rialto, Sibila* (Spain), *Sunday Times, Times Literary Supplement, Verse*.

'The Anaesthetist' was first published by Clarion Press, with lithographs by Valerie Mishin. 'Cover Version' was commissioned for the collection *After Ovid: New Metamorphoses*, edited by Michael Hofmann and James Lasdun (Faber and Faber/Farrar, Straus & Giroux, 1994).

All of the poems have been broadcast or transmitted on national network radio or television, on a variety of frequencies.

The Dead Sea Poems

And I was travelling lightly, barefoot
over bedrock, then through lands that were stitched
with breadplant and camomile. Or was it

burdock. For a living I was driving
a river of goats towards clean water,
when one of the herd cut loose to a cave

on the skyline. To flush it out, I shaped
a sling from a length of cotton bandage,
or was it a blanket, then launched a rock

at the target, which let out a racket –
the tell-tale sound of man-made objects.
Inside the cave like a set of skittles

stood a dozen caskets, and each one gasped –
a little theatrically perhaps –
when opened, then gave out a breath of musk

and pollen, and reaching down through cool sand
I found poems written in my own hand.
Being greatly in need of food and clothing,

and out of pocket, I let the lot go
for twelve times nothing, but saw them again
this spring, on public display, out of reach

under infra-red and ultra-sonic,
apparently worth an absolute packet.
Knowing now the price of my early art

I have gone some way towards taking it all
to heart, by bearing it all in mind, like
praying, saying it over and over

at night, by singing the whole of the work
to myself, every page of that innocent,
everyday, effortless verse, of which this

is the first.

The Anaesthetist

Hard to believe him when he trundles in,
scrubbed up and squeaky clean, manoeuvring
a handcart of deep-sea diving gear.

As crude as this after all these years:
the gown, the bottles and the hose, the tap,
the champagne gas, the stopwatch and the gloves,

the mask. As if it were extra,
filched from the air at random, at leisure –
hooking this hoof at the end of its trunk,

or planting one kiss from the bridge of the nose
to below the lips. Or legerdemain,
or sleight-of-hand to put them under,

to ask them to mumble from one to ten:
two is usual, three outstanding,
four is a miracle, by five he has them.

The giveaway signs – the pearls of the eyes.
In the palm of his hand, the valve, the throttle,
as he drops them down. A rule of thumb

is the ducking stool of nitrous oxide
for a duct or gland. For a limb or organ, either
a keel-haul of chloroform, a free-fall

of ether. They find themselves again
in houses, rooms, bend back to life
like willows after worshipping the flood;

they check their hands, their knees: still skin,
still blood, no worse, no better off for being
taken in. What must they make of him?

Man with a Golf Ball Heart

They set about him with a knife and fork, I heard,
and spooned it out. Dunlop, dimpled, perfectly hard.
It bounced on stone but not on softer ground – they made
a note of that. They slit the skin – a leathery,
rubbery, eyelid thing – and further in, three miles
of gut or string, elastic. Inside that, a pouch
or sac of pearl-white balm or gloss, like Copydex.
It weighed in at the low end of the litmus test
but wouldn't burn, and tasted bitter, bad, resin
perhaps from a tree or plant. And it gave off gas
that caused them all to weep when they inspected it.

That heart had been an apple once, they reckoned. Green.
They had a scheme to plant an apple there again
beginning with a pip, but he rejected it.

From the Middle Distance

I am found out
down south, holes pecked out for eyes and a mouth,
a scarecrow planted in a true square mile
of fallow ground.

Who set me up,
hammered this stake from the nape of my neck
to my left foot, down through the hips and ribs?
I think you did.

And the broomstick,
you cued it through the cuffs and sleeves, then lashed
the upright to the crosspiece at the heart,
then tied the hands.

That's how I stand.
And the black birds hang, waiting to feed
from the one tall thing in the flat of the land.
Well, here I am.

C.V.

Started, textiles, night shift,
no wheels, bussed it,
bus missed, thumbed it,
in my office sunbeam, fluffed it.

Shoe-shine, gofer, caddie,
bellboy, three bags full sir,
busker, juggler, bookie's runner,
move along there.

Sweatshop, mop and bucket,
given brush, shop floor,
slipped up, clocked in
half stoned, shown door.

Backwoodsman number, joiner,
timber, lumber, trouble,
axe fell, sacked for prank
with spirit-level bubble.

Sales rep, basic training,
car, own boss, P.A.,
commission, targets,
stuff that, cards same day.

Grant, small hours, square eyes,
half-arse O.U. student;
painting job, Forth Bridge,
but made redundant.

Understudy, back legs panto horse,
put down, not suited;
broke in Dr Martens
for police force, elbowed, booted.

Big break: trap shut, kickback,
fall guy, front man,
verbal contract, public admin,
quango stunt man,

collar felt, fair cop, threw hands in,
covered tracks up,
mea culpa, coughed, took flak
for every lash-up,

shredded trash, dug out top brass,
ate crap, digested orders,
sat on facts, last post
took rap for P.M.'s body odour;

rested, sick note,
self-certificated heart attack
but fit now, comeback,
job plan, welcome mat,

or out to grass, find door to lay me at.

I Say I Say I Say

Anyone here had a go at themselves
for a laugh? Anyone opened their wrists
with a blade in the bath? Those in the dark
at the back, listen hard. Those at the front
in the know, those of us who have, hands up,
let's show that inch of lacerated skin
between the forearm and the fist. Let's tell it
like it is: strong drink, a crimson tidemark
round the tub, a yard of lint, white towels
washed a dozen times, still pink. Tough luck.
A passion then for watches, bangles, cuffs.
A likely story: you were lashed by brambles
picking berries from the woods. Come clean, come good,
repeat with me the punch line 'Just like blood'
when those at the back rush forward to say
how a little love goes a long long long way.

White Christmas

For once it is a white Christmas,
so white that the roads are impassable
and my wife is snowbound
in a town untroubled by tractor or snowplough.
In bed, awake, alone. She calls

and we pass on our presents by telephone.
Mine is a watch, the very one
I would have chosen. Hers is a song,
the one with the line *Here come the hills of time*
and it sits in its sleeve,

unsung and unopened. But the dog downstairs
is worrying, gnawing, howling,
so I walk her through clean snow
along the tow-path to the boat-house at a steady pace,
then to my parents' place

where my mother is Marie Curie, in the kitchen
discovering radium, and my father is Fred Flintstone,
and a guest from the past has a look on her face meaning
lie and I'll have your teeth for a necklace, boy,
your eyeballs for earrings,

your bullshit for breakfast,
and my two-year-old niece is baby Jesus,
passing between us with the fruit of the earth
and the light of the world – Christingle – a blood orange
spiked with a burning candle.

We eat, but the dog begs at the table,
drinks from the toilet, sings in the cellar.
Only baby Jesus wanders with me down the stairs
with a shank of meat to see her, to feed her.
Later, when I stand to leave

my father wants to shake me by the hand
but my arms are heavy, made of a base metal,
and the dog wants to take me down the black lane, back
to an empty house again. A car goes by
with my sister inside

and to wave goodnight
she lifts the arm of the sleeping infant Christ,
but I turn my wrist to notice the time. There and then
I'm the man in the joke, the man in a world of friends
where all the clocks are stopped,

synchronising his own watch.

Before You Cut Loose,

                              put dogs on the list
of difficult things to lose. Those dogs ditched
on the North York Moors or the Sussex Downs
or hurled like bags of sand from rented cars
have followed their noses to market towns
and bounced like balls into their owners' arms.
I heard one story of a dog that swam
to the English coast from the Isle of Man,
and a dog that carried eggs and bacon
and a morning paper from the village
surfaced umpteen leagues and two years later,
bacon eaten but the eggs unbroken,
newsprint dry as tinder, to the letter.
A dog might wander the width of the map
to bury its head in its owner's lap,
crawl the last mile to dab a bleeding paw
against its own front door. To die at home,
a dog might walk its four legs to the bone.
You can take off the tag and the collar
but a dog wears one coat and one colour.
A dog got rid of – that's a dog for life.
No dog howls like a dog kicked out at night.
Try looking a dog like that in the eye.

A Hip Flask

To bring about safe passage to the States
and back, when taken from its sleeve or pouch
this gift sits where it should, tucked like a gun
inside the holster of a pocket, snug
against the leg or thigh or buttock, but
more suitably it fits the chest, the breast,
top left inside a jacket, where it feels
like armour plating or a sheriff's shield.

Good going for a little silver tin:
convex, concave, reflective on the out
and on the in. Misplaced, but then again
not knowing one malt from the next it's gin
that I'll be swigging, tipping to the lips
or sipping from the thimble of its lid.

I have a watch, map, toothbrush, cards and cash,
a licence, permit, pass, a ticket
going Eastern Seaboard, Central, Mountain
and Pacific,
            and a hip flask: tailored, weighed
and measured, worked both ways, this present made
to hide the heart and hold the heart in place.

Give

Of all the public places, dear,
to make a scene, I've chosen here.

Of all the doorways in the world
to choose to sleep, I've chosen yours.
I'm on the street, under the stars.

For coppers I can dance or sing.
For silver – swallow swords, eat fire.
For gold – escape from locks and chains.

It's not as if I'm holding out
for frankincense or myrrh, just change.

You give me tea. That's big of you.
I'm on my knees. I beg of you.

Stray

So you had to dine,
year in, year out, on a rusty chain
or salty washing line,

then chewed right through that makeshift tether
and one night strayed, still noosed
in a bitten-off length of leash and collar, sporting

a body that gnawed itself clear of the gallows,
burn marks, lesions to the skin,
that sort of thing.

Well, beginning tomorrow
you can feed for free at the butcher's bin
on festering meat and sickening marrow,

and take like a tramp
to the life of the street – go on,
get out – in bare feet.

Goalkeeper with a Cigarette

That's him in the green, green cotton jersey,
prince of the clean sheets – some upright insect
boxed between the sticks, the horizontal
and the pitch, stood with something up his sleeve,
armed with a pouch of tobacco and skins
to roll his own, or else a silver tin
containing eight or nine already rolled.
That's him with one behind his ear, between
his lips, or one tucked out of sight and lit –
a stamen cupped in the bud of his fist.
That's him sat down, not like those other clowns,
performing acrobatics on the bar, or press-ups
in the box, or running on the spot,
togged out in turtleneck pyjama-suits
with hands as stunted as a bunch of thumbs,
hands that are bandaged or swaddled with gloves,
laughable, frying-pan, sausage-man gloves.
Not my man, though, that's not what my man does;
a man who stubs his reefers on the post
and kicks his heels in the stud-marks and butts,
lighting the next from the last, in one breath
making the save of the year with his legs,
taking back a deep drag on the goal-line
in the next; on the one hand throwing out
or snaffling the ball from a high corner,
flicking off loose ash with the other. Or
in the freezing cold with both teams snorting
like flogged horses, with captains and coaches
effing and jeffing at backs and forwards,
talking steam, screaming exhausting orders,

that's not breath coming from my bloke, it's smoke.
Not him either goading the terraces,
baring his arse to the visitors' end
and dodging the sharpened ten-pence pieces,
playing up, picking a fight, but that's him
cadging a light from the ambulance men,
loosing off smoke rings, zeros or halos
that drift off, passively, over the goals
into nobody's face, up nobody's nose.
He is what he is, does whatever suits him,
because he has no highfalutin song
to sing, no neat message for the nation
on the theme of genius or dedication;
in his passport, under 'occupation',
no one forced the man to print the word
'custodian', and in *The Faber Book*
of Handy Hints his five-line entry reads:
'You young pretenders, keepers of the nought,
the nish, defenders of the sweet fuck-all,
think bigger than your pockets, profiles, health;
better by half to take a sideways view,
take a tip from me and deface yourselves.'

A Sculpture of Christ with Swings and a Slide

I found him like a fossil in the rock,
in the slab, waiting to be broken out.
Others I've chiselled have burst from the blocks
like genies from lamps, and one creature sprang

like a jack from a box. But not this one:
I took back the stone like flesh from a bone
while he dozed, sleeping it off on his cross.

The council bought him, stuck him in the park,
as out of place as a dog in a church.
The simple people came, told him secrets,
dressed him with flowers and polished his face,
put sweets in his mouth and gave him a name.
That's when I saw the thing these hands had made.

A Week and a Fortnight

Tricked into life with a needle and knife
but marked with the cross in the eye of a rifle,
laid from the first in the grave of a cradle.

Fed with the flesh not the fur of a peach
but bruised in the garden, tripped in the street,
bunged with a bottle of petrol and bleach.

Nursed at the breast on the cream of the nipple
but branded for keeps with the print of a fist,
buffed with a handkerchief, flannelled with spittle.

Baubled and bangled from ankle to wrist
but milked for a season, stung by a cousin,
dunked for a bet on the hob of an oven.

Picked for a prize for the fair of his face
but kicked to the foot from the head of the stairs,
buckled and belted and leathered and laced.

Spared from a stunt in the mouth of a lion
but dabbed on the foot with a soldering iron,
stabbed in the palm with a smouldering stub.

Left for an hour with booze and a razor
but carted by ambulance clear of the woods,
saved at the last by drugs and a laser.

Days for the dirty, life for the lost,
the acts of mercy and the stations of the cross,
the seven acts of mercy and the fourteen stations of the cross.

Dream Holiday

On the first night, a yawn,
the noiseless opening and closing of a downstairs door.
The dog lifted an ear,
and the next day the dog was kennelled in the car.

On the next night, a sneeze or cough
was shredded paper or a flash-gun going off.
The dog tapped its tail,
and the next night the dog was taken out and docked.

On the third night, footsteps in the roof-space
were bars of gold loaded into a suitcase.
The dog yelped,
and there and then the dog was muzzled with a belt.

On the fourth night, the Milky Way
was the gang of sparks from a nylon stocking lifted
from a face; water in the cistern
whispered, the dog whimpered;

toenails clipped were cables snipped, cracked knuckles
were connections uncoupled; splintered wood
and fractured glass, the dog shat,
and for that the dog was taken out and shot.

On the last night we were cleaned out,
the sound of tearing metal – hinges, locks –
drowned by the thought
of a dog asleep like a stone in its box.

On an Owd Piktcha

(from tJerman)

Int swelterin eet, mongst birds n tbeez,
side cool watter n rushes n reeds,
tChrahst Chahld sithee, born baht taint,
laikin arahnd on tVirgin's knee.

N pooakin its nooas aht o tleaves n tmoss,
already green, tTree o tCross.

C.B.

I should like to staff that radar station,
be the one man in its one-man operation,
tend its eighteen-nineteenths of an acre,
loaf some days in a lounging chair, read
Shakespeare.

In season
I might prune a tree or plant another,
lawn ninety degrees of the north-west corner,
rig up a spotlight – one, like a sunflower.

As well as this,
I should like to master the dials and discs,
trip the generator, throw the knife switch
with my good arm, so any charge would earth out
through my right side, not my heart.

But more to the point
I would shin up the mast and adjust the receiver,
align the ears of the saucers and dishes,
lend my mind to somebody's business:

bread vans, breakdowns, people on the air
from every pocket of the nation's surface,
cross-talk from the probation service.

Chapter and Verse

They were ushered along to the water's edge
to wait. Then one further back on the bank
said drink, so they drank, some of them
cupping their hands, taking the water like gods,
and some of them kneeling and lapping the water
like dogs.

And those that had sunk to their knees, gone down
on all fours, they were taken aside and tried
for stooping as low as a beast, but moreover
for kissing themselves on the lips in the lake.
They were all of them guilty and gathered together
and thumped. In the face. And those that were saved
were rewarded with mirrors and cups and praise
having made at the lake such a lasting impression.

Here endeth the first lesson.

Cover Version

How very fly of him,
the father of the skies,
to send his silver son
down on a thread of light

to drive a team of stirks
across the lower slopes
towards the shore, the sea.
A girl strolled on the beach.

Then leaving in a cloud
his three-pronged fork, he went
to ground, dressed as a stot,
a bull, and allocked there

and bezzled with the herd.
His hide was snod and bruff.
His coat was suede and soft
and chamois to the touch,

and white, as if one cut
would spill a mile of milk.
His eyes were made of moon.
His horns were carved in oak.

The girl was capped and feared,
would not go near at first,
then offered to his lips
a posy fit to eat.

He nuzzled at her fist,
then ligged down in the sand;
in turn she smittled him
with plants, then climbed his back,

at which he sammed her up
and plodged into the tide;
on, out, until they swammed
beyond the sight of land.

With him beneath she rode
the fields of surf, above
the brine, because the sea
might gag or garble her,

or gargle in her voice.
The waves have not the taste
of wine. A girl at sea
is never flush with choice.

Or, where they beached, they blent.
Or, where he covered her,
beneath a type of tree,
that tree was evergreen.

A Meteorite

So what, a piece of flint, a cinder, set
within the ring or pincers of my thumb
and index finger, like a precious stone.

Just so, precisely that, although
there's nothing other-worldly here, no hot
unstable element or compound, not
one point or dot or grain to place this rock
in outer space, no property or part
belonging to some other moon or star
known by a number rather than a name.

Not even a trace of Robinsonite,
unearthed in the Red Bird mercury mine
and christened by him whose crystalline find
was dust in his hand on coming to light.

But something all the same, for having flown
so far, found land, for having come to hand,
and put that way there's hardly anything
this piece can't say. A line of plot, a script,
and there and then this rock becomes a gem,
a gift; your fingers open, slowly, like
a flower, from a fist. As if. As if.

At the Quarantine Station

Far from the house the dog tastes the air,
turns tail and doubles back along its own tracks,
walking the way that only a dog walks:
that low-slung diagonal sideways scuttle,

the hind outpacing the front on the outside
almost. Back, I reckon, to the tidy yard
with churns and troughs given over to flowers;
across the cobbles and into its kennel.

The path runs west beside a wattle fence,
through a hedge, then breaks at ninety degrees to the left
to a shed in the shape of an aeroplane hangar,
beating its chest with its doors in the breeze,

the sound that had carried downwind for a mile
every night for a week. Lashing them shut,
I can't help but sneak a look inside,
and into the light like fish from the deep

come gross things: a pig on its knees, unclean, a ram
with a tail from its head and horns at the rear end,
a goat on its last legs, the feet not cloven but webbed,
cattle in pairs, skewbald in leather and suede

and joined at the ribs, a horse in its stall,
fully formed, no more than two or three hands tall . . .
To make for home direct involves a steeplechase
of barbed-wire fences, five-bar gates

and ankle-breaking stones in every ditch.
I'm thinking, someone hasn't heard the last of this.

D-notice

To say the least, I should like that
very much indeed. To start with,
have less of the thing the cat
cleans its arse with,

roll it back like a red carpet.
To ease out the cork from the neck
now and then – not for speaking though,
for breathing.

Or make like a pumpkin, I mean
cut out the cheek, leave out
the lip. As for the teeth, keep them
together, clean.

To go without saying, that would
be extremely seemly. To tie
the tongue instead of wagging it,
clamp the jaw, put

a sock and not a foot in it,
do the soft pedal, not a mile
a minute. Give it a rest,
a thumb, a breast,

save my breath to cool my porridge,
bung the hole with a spoon, a plum,
open wide – not for preaching though,
for feeding.

To hold my noise for ever, that
would be my pleasure. To bite back,
track the tongue and trap it, let
the cat have it.

Next time I'll know. Next time
I'll hold this tongue in line, I'll keep
this blabbermouth of mine in mind.
And let it lie.

The Two of Us

(after Laycock)

You sat sitting in your country seat
with maidens, servants waiting hand and foot.
You eating swan, crustaceans, starters, seconds, sweet.
You dressed for dinner, worsted, made to measure. Cut:
me darning socks, me lodging at the gate,
me stewing turnips, beet, one spud,
a badger bone. Turf squealing in the grate –
no coal, no wood.

No good. You in your splendour: leather,
rhinestone, ermine, snakeskin, satin, silk,
a felt hat finished with a dodo feather.
Someone's seen you swimming lengths in gold-top milk.
Me parched, me in a donkey jacket,
brewing tea from sawdust mashed in cuckoo spit,
me waiting for the peaks to melt, the rain to racket
on the metal roof, the sky to split,

and you on-stream, piped-up, plugged-in, you worth a mint
and tighter than a turtle's snatch.
Me making light of making do with peat and flint
for heat, a glow-worm for a reading lamp. No match.
The valleys where the game is, where the maize is –
yours. I've got this plot just six foot long
by three foot wide, for greens for now, for daisies
when I'm dead and gone.

You've got the lot, the full set:
chopper, Roller, horse-drawn carriage, microlight, skidoo,
a rosewood yacht, a private jet.
I'm all for saying that you're fucking loaded, you.
And me, I clomp about on foot from field to street;
these clogs I'm shod with, held together now with segs
and fashioned for my father's father's father's feet –
they're on their last legs.

Some in the village reckon we're alike, akin:
same neck, same chin. Up close that's what they've found,
some sameness in the skin,
or else they've tapped me on the back and you've turned round.
Same seed, they say, same shoot,
like I'm some cutting taken from the tree,
like I'm some twig related to the root.
But I can't see it, me.

So when it comes to nailing down the lid
if I were you I wouldn't go with nothing.
Pick some goods and chattels, bits and bobs like Tutankhamen did,
and have them planted in the coffin.
Opera glasses, fob-watch, fountain pen, a case of fishing flies,
a silver name-tag necklace full-stopped with a precious stone,
a pair of one pound coins to plug the eyes,
a credit card, a mobile phone,

some sentimental piece of earthenware,
a collar stud, a cufflink and a tiepin,
thirteen things to stand the wear and tear
of seasons underground, and I'll take what I'm standing up in.
That way, on the day they dig us out
they'll know that you were something really fucking fine
and I was nowt.
Keep that in mind,

because the worm won't know your make of bone from mine.

Afterword

Fact: the world will be fixed
in the eyes of friends
who head out west and fetch up
back at home again.

It's that Einstein thing
where one of two twins
takes off for a spin
and returns in the spring

to the place of his birth
with a gift for his brother.
And they see for themselves,
each eyeing the other

through a telescope now
which had once been a mirror.

Five Eleven Ninety Nine

The makings of the fire to end all fires,
the takings of the year, all kinds of cane
and kindling to begin with, tinder sticks,
the trunk and branches of a silver birch

brought down by lightning, dragged here like a plough
through heavy earth from twenty fields away.
Timber: floorboards oiled and seasoned, planking,
purlins, sleepers, pelmets, casements, railings,

sacks of sweepings, splinters, sawdust, shavings.
Items on their own: a fold-away bed,
an eight-foot length of four-by-two, a pew,
a tea chest – empty, three piano legs,

a mantelpiece and a lazy Susan,
a table-top, the butt of a shotgun,
a toilet-seat, two-thirds of a triptych,
a Moses basket with bobbins in it,

a pair of ladders, half a stable-door,
a stump, one stilt, the best part of a boat,
a sight-screen stolen from the cricket field,
a hod, a garden bench, a wagon wheel.

We guess the place, divine it, dig a hole
then plant and hoist and pot the centre pole –
tall, redwood-size, of the telegraph type,
held tight with guy-ropes, hawsers, baling wire –

and for a week it has to stand alone,
stand for itself, a mark, a line of sight,
a stripe against the sky. Steeple, needle,
spindle casting half a mile of shadow

at dusk, at dawn another half-mile more.
Held down, held firm, but not to climb or scale;
strung, stayed, but with an element of play –
in wind the top nods inches either way.

Thing to surround, build around, or simply
the solid opposite of a chimney.
Symbol, signal, trigger for those people
who deliver all things combustible

this time of year, who rummage through attics
and huts, cellars and sheds, people who check
the yards and feet and inches of their lives
for something safe to sacrifice, figures

who visit the site, arrive with a box
and set it down like a child's coffin, or
those who come after dark, before first light,
with black bags that are bursting with something

and nothing. Rolls of oilcloth are carted
by hand. A furlong of carpet appears
that must have been brought here by van. Some kid
comes a mile and a third, uphill, to tip

a hundredweight of paper from a pram,
and a man turns up to empty a bin,
does so, picks through the garbage, finds a thing
or two — a ball of string, a leather shoe —

loads up and takes his findings home with him.
Later still that man comes back with a loose
half-full half-empty sack of low-grade coal —
offensive now within this smokeless zone —

and lugs it, wears it draped around his neck
like a dead foal, one hand hold of each end,
then on his knee he lays it down. Two coals
run out like two rats across the hard ground.

Such comings, givings, goings. Morning finds
the pole upstanding through a tractor tyre —
half a ton, those, so how did that get there?
All else scattered, as if dropped from the air,

litter brought from somewhere else to right here
by hurricane or twister, washed ashore and beached
by long-shore drift and gale-force winds
and a hard night of high seas. Flotsam. Dreck.

We stack the fire at the eleventh hour,
begin by propping staves and leaning splints
against the centre-piece, build up and out
from slats and rafters through to joists and beams,

take notice of its changing shape: a cairn
becoming wigwam, then becoming dome,
becoming pyramid, then bell, then cone.
It has its features: priest-holes, passageways,

a box-room, alcoves, doors. We hide and hoard,
stack bales of paper steeped in paraffin
within its walls, stow blankets doused in oil,
load every seam with goods – goods to take hold –

and thread each flash point with a length of rope
soaked through with petrol, kerosene or meths
and trail the loose end to a distant place.
Unnecessary, but a nice touch, though.

That moment, then, before the burning starts –
like waiting for the tingle in the track
before the train, or on the empty road
before the motorcade, the time it takes

each elephant to wander from lightning
to thunder. That, or something in the bones
or in the weather, on the wind, a twinge
within the works of some barometer,

shouts of timber in the coral canyon
of the ear, the smell of burning pouring
through the chambers of the nose, a voltage
in the lochs and groves of tubes and glands. Hands

hang fire, hang loose in pairs of leather gloves,
and coolant flows and fills the trunks and roots
and limbs and leaves and needles of the lungs.
Then someone makes a move, a match gets struck . . .

The hiss first of damp wood, the fizz of steam,
a water-coloured flame, cradled and cupped
in a sheltered place, then circled and snuffed
by a twist of smoke. Something else flares up,

then chokes – a flame blown out by its own breath –
and a third and fourth are checked. More smoke
without fire, then a further space alive
with light, a chamber deep inside aglow

for good this time, fuelled with the right stuff,
feeding on something loose for long enough
to tempt another thing to burn, combust,
to spread its word, to chatter its own name

through a stook of canes, to start a whisper
here and there that spreads across the broad base,
a rumour handed down, passed round and shared.
Heat dealt to every point, backed up by flames.

Sounds – the popping of corn, cars back-firing.
And sharps and flats, affricates, fricatives,
screams, an acetylene torch igniting,
a pilot light – its circular breathing.

The animal squeal of air escaping.
Snapping of soft wood – the bones of babies.
The depth-charge of a blown-out metal drum.
A pressurized can goes off like a gun,

at which a fox cuts loose from the fire, there
then gone, having waited this long to bolt
like a ball of light that breaks from the skin
of the sun; that makes it then dies. Like so,

observed through special telescopes, that is.
Lit from the front, the faces we wear
are masks, and bare hands hang down from their cuffs
like lamps. Heat to our hearts, but we each feel

the bite of frost from the nape of the neck
to the heels, a cold current through the spine
despite a hugging of duds: Russian dolls –
two shirts, three jumpers, jacket, anorak,

topped by an uncle's outsize overcoat.
A lending of heat and light to the air
but splinters of ice in our hands and hair.
Nothing to swing the weather vane, no breeze,

but down an avenue of silent trees
a dog walks a man through a rain of leaves.
Far detail: a goods-train hauling road-stone
wheel-spins at a set of signals. Diesel.

An hour later, though, the fire deep-seated,
up to speed, at full tilt. A garage roof,
bituminous, slides forward in the heat.
A window pops from its frame. A small girl

paddles in the puddle of her own boots,
melted to her feet. A man with an oar
comes foward from the crowd with a bauble
or a silver orb on its outstretched blade –

a cooking apple cased in baking foil –
which he expertly lays at the white heart
of the flames. 'For eating, later,' he says,
then stabs the fire and swipes the leading edge

of the burning oar no more than an inch
or so from the hat on the balding head
of his brother-in-law. Then shoulders it,
carries it like a banner, turns around,

and then ditches it, pitches it forward;
the sharp end finds the earth, digs in, goes out.
A grown man blisters his fingers and screams.
And a wet dog sings in a cloud of steam.

A man who is blind walks down from his hill,
through the woods, having sensed a form of light
on his eyes when he raised his head, and heard
convected cinders raining on his roof.

A decent blaze, he says, but a shadow
of those in the past, of course, in the days
when smoke was mistaken for night, when fires
would singe an eyebrow from a mile away

or roast a chestnut hanging on its branch
or brown the skin through several layers of clothes.
One year his sister wore a floral blouse;
the next that she knew she was tanned with shapes

of bluets, goosefoot and morning glory.
Fires so full of the sun that each brought on
a second spring, an autumn flowering
of lilies, sesame and panic grass

and feverfew. And sickle senna too.
Another year a farmer drove a herd
of bullocks through the flames, and some came through
unscathed, but others fell, and ribs and steaks

were there to eat for those who wanted them.
But worst, the season he remembers most,
when seven children in a paper chase
holed up inside the mound of bric-a-brac

to be fired that night, and slept. And the rest
was a case of identification
by watches and lockets, fillings and teeth.
Someone gets the man a drink, and a seat.

And buildings swim in the haze of the heat.
And rockets set out for parks and gardens
and nose-dive into purple streets. And sparks
make the most of some moments of stardom.

And flakes of ash and motes of soot float up,
cool down, fall out, then go to ground. No sign,
no trace, unless they settle on the skin,
unless they come to hand or find a face

to brush or smudge or dust or break against.
And panes of glass take a shine to the fire,
and glass to all sides is amazed with light,
and every surface of a similar type

carries a torch, becomes inflamed. And eyes
if they blink are ablaze on the inside.
Gunpowder battles it out in the sky
where rockets go on unzipping the night.

Two or three at a time each firework blooms,
flowers and fruits with sodium yellows
and calcium reds, shades of strontium
and copper – copper green and copper blue.

The tease of a paper fuse, then gunsmoke
shot with potash fumes, and cordite nosing
out of every empty barrel, casing,
tube. And several figures surround each squib,

and each and every huddle of people,
adults and kids, is the cast and crew
of its own short film, fifteen seconds long
at most and flickering – not black and white

but tinted in tones of alloys and chromes.
A soundtrack of sibilants, clacks and clicks,
and thuds and shrieks that are harder to place –
warfare or birdsong, peacocks or bombshells,

air raids, kittiwakes. And familiar sights,
like a Catherine wheel escaping its tail,
a Roman candle that snowballs the moon.
Clear skies, a night with its lid taken off

but peppered and strafed with fractals and flak,
gerbes and Saxons, star shells, Mines of Serpents,
Bengal Lights and other coruscations,
and the fire, glazing every act and scene

with versions of orange and tangerine,
the woods to the east thrown over with pink
and with crimson. There are cats in those woods,
they reckon, wild ones. Cats, and also mink,

but no one alive to swear they've seen them.
And a wheel of cheese – the moon on the rise,
caught like a ball in the branches of trees.
And a heat so solid now, a hard glow

we take for granted, easy come and go,
light years away from the seasons of flint
and stone and steel and smoke and leaves, the times
of trees ignited by bolts of lightning,

the untouchable gold of lava flow,
stories of sparks more precious than pearls
thrown up from the hooves of careering colts
or buffalo, struck from the beaks and claws

of eagles and hawks, and the days of flames
kept secret and safe in temples and caves.
Fire borrowed from neighbours and given back,
caught from the burning tail of a wild cat,

brought from the sun in the beak of a wren
or got from the glint in a precious gem.
Or fire snapped like twigs from red-berried trees,
bought from the otherworld, sought in the hearts

of warm-blooded things, under the stoat's tongue,
pulled from the nail of an old woman's thumb.
A distant cry from this whiteness of heat,
as easily raised as falling asleep.

But then by one degree the brightness fades.
A fraction at first, it has to be said,
but then again the sun must pass its best
and move through noon the second that it strikes,

and in the space it takes to check a watch
another inch of time gets dropped, slides by,
is lost. The way it is with peaks and troughs —
that's how it goes with Fahrenheit and clocks.

So we look to ourselves for something to burn,
to slow up the countdown of Centigrade,
but come up with metal: bedsteads and prams,
chains and a kettle, a bicycle frame.

A team of brothers walk further afield
to check the meadows of the north-north-east,
to comb the copse to the west of the creek,
to trawl for driftwood on the lakeside beach,

to haul the sunken jetty from the tarn,
then make a final circle of the town
and lift the stacks of litter from the streets.
They amble back with the following things:

a sack of potatoes going to seed,
a peacock feather, the skull of a sheep.
Thrown on, the feather shrinks then disappears,
the sack of spuds rolls over, waters, weeps;

with flames for eyes, the skull keeps its own shape.
Someone has to be to blame, so a man
who hasn't pulled his weight, who feeds his face
with coffee and cake is taken away.

We gather round, close in. In steel-cap boots
and a boiler-suit the friend of a friend
turns amber embers over with a spade,
splits wood in search of heat, looks for a pulse

within the charred remains of logs and stumps.
A girl who is said to be deaf and dumb
comes forward with a pitch-fork and a brush
and turns and sweeps the margins of the flames

for seeds and knots and crumbs, chippings and thorns
that fizz and fry an inch above the heat,
then stops, then looks, then javels both the tools
into a fire that isn't hot enough

to detonate the bristles of the brush
or separate the two halves of the fork
by rapidly unseasoning the splice.
She backs off to a darker place, resigned.

We stand in profile, figures from an age
before the dawn, paintings on a cave wall,
a people waiting for a word or sign,
one of the tribe to whisper something like

when one thing dies begin again inside;
look for it in the heartbeat of the tide,
wade in the coves and bays along the coast,
between the toes. Plot the zones and borders,

map the suburbs, boroughs, claim the polders,
sift the rapids five or six times over,
trace the water courses, mark the passes
and the gorges, plant and farm the ocean,

mow the steppes and fens and string the bridges
out between the contours of the ridges,
pick and pluck the cobweb of the matrix
of the districts, fly, align the air-strips,

take a section, make a transit, chart it,
pan the Gulf Stream, dive, way beneath the hull,
then rise towards the light until the head
comes up against the ice-cap of the skull.

But we have given all of what we own
and what we are, and it has come to this:
this place, this date, this time, these tens of us,
all free but shadowless and primitive,

no more than silhouettes or negatives
or hieroglyphics, stark and shivering.
A half-life, heat-loss at a rate of knots,
an hour at most before the very last.

All lost. Until it dawns on one of us
to make the most of something from the past.
He walks us to a garage, picks the lock
and pinpoints with a torch a heavy cloth,

asbestos, woven, terrible to touch,
then covering his mouth against the dust
that hangs like plankton in the beam of light
he drags the cloth away to find a cross.

No time for measuring the shortest straw
or drawing lots. There's mention of a name,
and singled out the strongest of us bends
and takes its length along his spine, its frame

an early aeroplane as someone says,
and takes its width across his arms and neck,
its point of balance screwing down his head
to face his feet, then walks, or rather wades,

bent double, blinkered, heavy-eyed, not blind,
not blessed with sight, half bird, half vertebrate,
not troubled with the gift of flight, dead weight,
not given to the open sky. Not right.

We guide him to the left towards the site
through ginnels where his wing-span clips the sides
of houses, makes a xylophone of pipes
and railings, drum-rolls on a picket fence

and likewise once again along a length
of paling, then through parkland, puddles, sludge,
the tail-end ploughing, paying out a groove
between his footprints planted in the mud,

then onto concrete paving where he halts
above a hopscotch pattern sketched in chalk.
And there he falls, but stands up straight and walks
beneath a window where his mother waves

and calls his name, warns him to tie his boots
or fall again. He climbs a dozen steps,
then rests, by leaning with his arm outstretched,
hand flat against a wall. For a short while

we take the strain, but he loads up again
and makes for the faint light at the far end
of the lane, where a woman seems to wait
to produce a handkerchief trimmed with lace

from inside her sleeve, and to wipe his face.
He falls a second time and then a third,
but rounds the final corner on his knees
and finds his feet when he sees the remains

of the light and heat, and raises the cross
to its full height, and hugs it like a bear.
Upright, it seems to stand for something there.
Whatever he wears is filthy and torn,

the pins and needles of splinters and spells
are under his nails and deep in his hands
like thorns. And when he tears himself away
it stays, held up by nothing more than air.

However, mass like that, the sort, weighed flat,
to break a back or trip a heart attack,
amounts to next to nothing stacked; a hair
can trigger it, a tap from something slight

can topple it, say timber and it tips.
In this case someone serves up half a brick
that clips the crosspiece on the left-hand arm;
it twists, turns face about, tilts and quickens,

mimics the act of launching a discus,
the east and west of its cardinal points
beginning to roll, its axis falling
out of centre, out of true. Then it lands –

a noiseless splashdown in a pool of ash
invoking a mushroom of sparks and chaff
that takes its time to winnow and settle,
to clear. Hats in the air, and a loud cheer.

And it simmers and stews in its own steam,
then ignites. Those expecting an incense
of palm and cedar, the scent of olive
and cypress, are surprised by the odour

of willow and oak and pine and alder,
resins and oils from the Colne and Calder
that witter and whine as they brush with fire.
Warmth for an hour, but not a minute more.

And blackness follows every burst of flames
that leaves us cold again, hands pocketed,
outdone, outshone, left in the shade by stars
that boil with light when the dark inflames them,

put to shame by shapes and constellations
that were dead and countersunk and buried,
hammered home in deep space. Like the new view
of the full moon, on full beam, in full bloom,

the open silver flower of the moon,
the boulder of the moon or the moon's shield,
hallmarked with valleys and rivers and fields,
the streams and snakes and fossils of the moon,

the long plumbago nights and graphite days,
the mercury seas and mercury lakes
of the moon, the moon on a plate, the date
and the name and the make of the full moon.

Under which we figure out the next move.
Off to the west, at the boarding kennels,
low down in the fringe of the sky, level
with chimneys, the crowns of trees and pylons,

a star, four-sided, breaks the horizon –
light in the shape of a dormer window –
and out of its frame a man emerges,
naked and bald and mad, head and shoulders,

and says his piece, shouts the odds about dogs
and vomit, fools returning to folly,
and the hounds in his keeping fratch and fret
or clatter the mesh of his twelve-foot fence.

And on the one hand someone rattles off
the preconditions, lists them one by one:
for little, wedding, middle, index, thumb,
read pressure, discharge, friction, action, heat

of any kind. But on the other hand
the things we're up against: clay, fibro, lime,
the silicates and tungstates, certain salts
and sodas, borax, alum; more than five,

not counting water and things of that kind.
Scissors cut paper and paper wraps rock,
rock blunts the scissors but water, water
swamps and dulls and rusts and dampens the lot.

Nothing else for it. The tightest of men
makes a move for his wallet, goes through it
for fivers, tenners and twenty-pound notes
and lets them drift to the little that's left

of the incandescence, like petals, picked
for the purpose of proving love, or not.
Another takes a last look through a deck
of snapshots, passport-size, in black and white,

then deals that pack of thirteen photographs
to the fire, the way some poker player
sits and tosses cards into a cocked hat.
And each image burns with a true colour.

Another burns a book of stamps, a cheque,
a calling-card, goes through his pockets, finds
and flings a ticket stub, a serviette,
a driving licence, birth certificate.

Another pulls a hip flask from his side,
empties it out on a mound of briquette;
the liquid vaporizes into scent:
angelica, wormwood, star-anise, mint.

He turns to us and tells us what it is
or what it was, and then pockets the flask.
Another strips his friend of his flat cap,
prizes it from him like a bottle top,

then slings it, frisbee-style, into the ash.
Another man decapitates himself
or so it looks from here, beheads himself,
it seems, unzips the detachable hood

from his coat for the sake of the lost cause,
looks for a naked flame, and on it goes.
And on it goes: a pair of gloves, a scarf,
a balaclava lifted from a face.

The act of keeping warm by burning clothes —
like eating your own hand to stay alive
or tapping your arm for a quart of blood
to survive. Tell that to the starving, though,

and the dry, those of us feeling the cold
tonight. We follow suit, burn every stitch
for one last wave of heat, pixel of light.
Unbuttoned but thankfully out of sight

except in the eye of the moon, silent
except for the padding of feet, bare feet,
we turn to go, then go together, home
in numbers, then in pairs and then alone

to houses that are empty, frozen, stone,
to rooms that are skeletal, stripped, unmade,
uncurtained windows, doorways open wide,
to beds without cover, lamps without shade.

At dawn, through living daylight, half asleep,
we drift back to the place, which brings to mind
a crater punched home by a meteorite
or else a launch-pad or a testing-site.

Kicking through the feather-bed of ashes
someone flushes out a half-baked apple.
Softened, burnt and blistered on the skin, but
hardly touched within. Inedible thing,

the flesh gone muddy, foul, the core and pips
that no one cares to eat still fresh, still ripe,
and him who found it heads off down the slope
towards the park and plants or buries it.

We wait, listless, aimless now it's over,
ready for what follows, what comes after,
stood beneath an iron sky together,
awkwardly at first, until whenever.